GARDEN FOR BIRDS

by Nigel Matthews
illustrations by Tessa Lovatt-Smith

CONTENTS

		page
1.	**Introduction** - realistic encouragement	3
2.	**Sharing your home with the birds** - meeting the needs of different birds	4
3.	**Garden habitats for all** - lawns, flower borders, trees, shrubs, hedgerow, climbers and ponds	8
4.	**Water, water everywhere**... - for drinking, bathing and freshwater food	22
5.	**Little extras** - the heaps, piles, stumps and perches that could make all the difference	26
6.	**Unusual gardening tips** - pests, children and birds, if you can't beat them, join them!	30
7.	**Bird pests and predators** - understanding and overcoming bird problems	34
8.	**Dinner is served** - artificial food: how, what and when to provide	37
9.	**House to Let** - nesting and nest boxes	42
	Appendices - common garden birds, addresses, books etc.	47-48

SGC Books

GARDEN FOR BIRDS

by © Nigel Matthews

First Published 1992 by
S G C Books, PO Box 49, Spalding, Lincs PE11 1NZ
Telephone: (0775) 769518

Cataloguing in Publication Data is available from *The British Library*

ISBN 1-85116-805-2

About the author...

Nigel Matthews is currently Head of Education at the Kent Trust for Nature Conservation. Having gained a PhD from research on the feeding habits of bullfinches, he set up a field studies centre in Kent. A bird watcher from an early age, and now licensed as a bird ringer, Nigel has come into close contact with thousands of birds and is particularly keen to encourage others to learn about, appreciate and care for them. This desire is reflected in his writing, his talks to both young and old, and in his enthusiastic leadership of wildlife activities, in field, wood and garden.

Conservation on both sides of the garden fence

Many people manage without any garden at all. Happy, though, are those who do have one, for it is perhaps in the garden that many children have their first introduction to nature. It is here that appreciation of the whole world around us begins, and if we don't appreciate, we won't care...then we are on a very slippery garden path indeed, one that endangers not only the wild animals and plants around us, but ultimately our own existence too.

We must all realise the value of conservation: locally, nationally and globally. The fact is that, ultimately, we depend on wildlife just as much as wildlife depends on us! All life is inextricably linked, like a complex but delicate web. Destroy the web and we, or our children, will suffer.

We must all play our part, not only in our gardens but by educating neighbours and relatives and by supporting conservation organisations as they work to protect and manage habitats for wildlife throughout the world.

---

1 INTRODUCTION

This is a book for people who both like birds and have at least partial control of a garden, be it at home, school or work. We take a look at the lives of birds and their needs at different times of year and measure this against what we as gardeners can provide.

In this day and age when our wildlife is under constant threat from a great assortment of mostly man-made dangers, it can only be a very good thing when a decision to garden for birds is made. We really can help the birds.

Our choice of home usually depends more on the house than the garden; for birds it is the other way round. From the outset it is as well to bear in mind that unless your garden is particularly large, your ability to attract birds will depend as much on the nature of the neighbours' land as on anything you can do on your patch. This is not accepting defeat before even starting, but merely stating the facts so as to enable the bird-friendly gardener to be realistic in his or her expectations. Indeed, on a positive note, to peer over the garden fence is perhaps the first thing to do!
Go on, have a look ... what do you see?

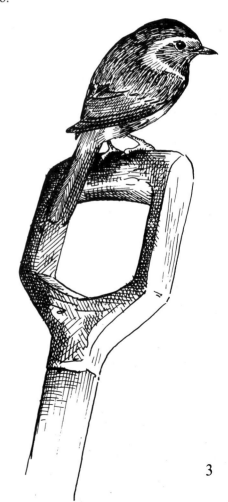

If you see a wood nearby, then you are in for a treat, for many woodland birds make regular sorties into suitable garden habitats; some will take up almost permanent residence. If you live next to a field, then be prepared for fewer summertime breeding birds, perhaps more winter visitors and certainly many birds out in the field. If, like most of us, your garden is surrounded by other gardens, houses and streets then take up the challenge of creating, in your 'back yard', a first-class haven for what will be, for the most part, the commoner but no less fascinating species.

Remember that gardening for birds is much more than an attempt to increase the species 'tick list'. It involves trying to understand the birds, devising ways of encouraging them to venture close to the house, providing suitable nest sites and a whole range of other considerations. Perhaps most importantly, it includes enjoying the birds, their plumage, their behaviour, their very presence in what most people regard as their own garden. **From here on consider your plot of land, whether or not you think it has great promise as a bird garden, as being under joint ownership.**

Don't be selfish, share it.

Whether or not you approve of the concept of sharing your home with the birds, the birds themselves will already have taken this for granted. Furthermore their view of sharing is somewhat different from ours!

Three basic necessities

In considering the needs of birds, it is helpful to compare these with what people need. Both lists obviously vary with circumstances like age, but can be simplified as follows:

Food

Like human babies, nestlings require a high-protein diet, especially during their first few days. Parent of most garden birds, even seed-eating species such as finches and sparrows, hunt for insects or other invertebrate animals for their young. For the 'vegetarians', the proportion of animal food on the menu declines gradually as feathers and muscles grow.

The 'baby' and 'child' stages in garden birds are relatively short. A sparrow spends only 15 days in the nest and is almost fully grown when it flies. Two or three weeks later the young bird can fend for itself; indeed by this time the parents may well have started on their next brood!

As we shall see, full-grown birds often specialise in particular foods but, like people, need variety and balance for a healthy life.

Plumage

A bird's feathers are its clothes, and must protect it in all weathers, day and night, summer and winter. Water birds have specially waterproof feathers but even land birds have rainproof plumage. Most garden birds change (or moult) their feathers once a year in the early autumn; they are then well covered for the winter.

As with people, appearance is most important in birds' pairing and mating behaviour. Male birds are generally more colourful than females, and often their courtship displays show off their plumage to the best possible effect. Freshly-grown feathers of some birds, including finches, sparrows and buntings, are tipped with drab buffs or browns. However, these tips wear off through the winter, revealing brighter colours beneath, in time for the breeding season.

Summer ♂ *Winter ♂* *Chaffinch* ♀

Summer *Winter* *Reed Bunting*

A house

In many ways a bird's nest fulfils the same purpose as a person's house. The nest provides shelter for eggs, young and even the brooding parent. Great skill is needed to make it strong, well insulated from cold, and well hidden from predators. It is a base from which the parents forage and is regarded as a place of safety by the nestlings; many leap out into the big wide world very reluctantly indeed!

The great difference between our house and a bird's nest is the length of time for which it is used. In our case, we live our whole life around the house, but birds use their nests almost solely for breeding. Even the vast majority of young birds on their first night out find a new 'bed' to sleep in.

These basic necessities are the key to successful gardening for birds. The best bird gardens offer food for both young birds and old; they help in the vital business of feather care and provide both material and suitable sites for nesting.

5

Home-grown food for all

One obvious question is, what foods do adult birds require? Let's start with the concept of home-grown, native foods.

Before people modified the environment for their own benefit, birds had only 'natural', native foods to eat. Seed-eating birds had only the seeds of wild plants; those that ate buds had no cultivated pear trees to feed from and so on. However, in our quest for a comfortable life, we have not only allowed agriculture, houses, roads and other developments to dominate the landscape, but we have also introduced a vast array of plants from other parts of the world to our towns, work-places and gardens. These non-native plants in turn support at least a small selection of animals which would not otherwise survive here. Thus the 20th Century British bird is confronted with a menu of great length, perhaps nowhere more so than in a modern garden.

Since gardens are, in evolutionary terms, a relatively new habitat, garden birds must be adaptable. However, the problem is that many insects (especially their immature stages) feed on only a small range of plants. Indeed some will eat, say leaves, from only a single species of plant (such as the small tortoiseshell butterfly whose caterpillar feeds only on stinging nettles).
Such insects are unable to live in areas without their particular native food plant.

It follows that although non-native nectar-rich plants attract hordes of adult insects to feed, a garden without a selection of native shrubs and trees is indeed impoverished. Compare the native with the introduced trees and shrubs in the table below, and the case is proved beyond doubt. Having said this, non-native trees and shrubs often have large numbers of the few insect species they host!

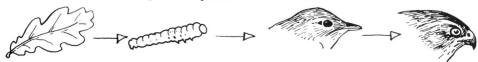

The best trees for insects

This list shows how some trees and shrubs have many more kinds of insects associated with them than others. These insects include all the various insect families (i.e. not just moths and butterflies).

Tree or shrub * indicates non-native species.	No of insect species
Oaks, Willows, Birch,	over 200
Hawthorn, Blackthorn	up to 200
Poplars, Aspen, Crab apple, Scots pine, Alder, Elm, Hazel, Beech, Ash, Spruce*, Lime, Hornbeam, Rowan, Maple, Juniper	20 - 100
Larch*, Fir*, Sycamore*, Holly, Sweet chestnut*, Horse chestnut*, Yew, Walnut*, Holm oak*, Plane*	less then 20

Remember that for a garden to be rich in birds it must also be rich in other wildlife. Home-grown food for all means food for plants, food for mini- and maxi-beasts of many kinds ... and thus food for birds. If you are really successful you'll attract a bird-eating bird!

6

Vegetarian birds

Although not normally applied to birds, the term 'vegetarian' does suggest a diet of plants and plant products, and finches, sparrows and buntings certainly fit into this category for much of the time. Like vegetarian people, birds select the more nutritious plant parts to eat: seeds, fruits, buds, shoots, seedlings, flowers, nectar, and relatively rarely leaves or twigs.

finches have stout, seed-eating bills

By definition, potential vegetable food cannot escape, but it may well hide or protect itself. Thus seeds may be encased in a hard nut, buds surrounded by tough scales and leaves laced with unpalatable chemicals which in quantity would poison a bird! On the other hand, many plants now rely on birds to disperse their seeds. They therefore embed the seeds in attractive fleshy fruits which the birds eat whole. The seeds are later deposited, ready for germination, some distance away in the birds' droppings.

Vegetarian birds often form winter flocks on open fields and other apparently desolate places. Here they search for the dwindling stock of dormant seeds on the soil's surface. The bird gardener's answer to their plight is, first, a supply of seed-bearing plants in the flower border purposely left 'untidy', and second, the bird table.

Carnivorous birds

For simplicity it is useful to consider birds which prefer animal food under this heading. These include birds of prey, those that catch worms, and especially those that eat insects, spiders and other invertebrates.

Unlike plants, few animals benefit from being caught and eaten, so each animal species has its ways of escaping attention. Butterflies have erratic flight, caterpillars are usually well camouflaged, many invertebrates feed only at night and many others burrow deep into wood or soil.

warblers have fine insect-eating bills

Although most insect specialists migrate south for the winter, birds like the wren, long-tailed tit and goldcrest are in our gardens all year round. To help these, provide a thick bushy or woodland-edge habitat in which insects and their eggs, larvae and pupae can be found.

Omnivorous birds

The trouble with specialising in a particular diet is that few foods are continuously plentiful. It's fine being a finch in autumn when all the plants have set seeds in abundance, but not in early spring when the few seeds that remain germinate! Take a walk in the snow and look for animal food and the problems faced by a carnivore are clear.

Apart from migrating, the other basic answer to this problem is a change of diet, to eat whatever is available at any given time of year, i.e. to be omnivorous. Many garden birds fit best in this category, including thrushes for example, which readily eat fruit and bird table scraps when soil invertebrates run short. The crow family is another good example; their diet ranges from nestling birds to seeds.

the magpie will eat almost anything

7

3 | GARDEN HABITATS FOR ALL

A habitat is defined as the natural home of an animal or plant. The bird gardener's aim should therefore be to manage the plants, trees, fences, paths, patio and pond to create a range of habitats which feel 'just like home' for many birds.

Lawn or meadow

An ordinary mown lawn, cut to say 5-10 cm, is a valuable feeding habitat for thrushes, the starling, dunnock, pied wagtail ... even the green woodpecker.

However, establishing a wild-flower meadow on part of the lawn will add beauty and colour to the outlook, and provide a wealth of nectar, seeds and larval insect food plants which will directly or indirectly benefit other birds.

Either a spring or summer meadow is worth attempting without adding any additional plants especially around trees; even seeding dandelions attract finches to feed. However, you will probably want to add some new species.

Spring meadow	Summer meadow	Either
Birds-foot-trefoil	Field scabious	Ribwort plantain
Selfheal	Black knapweed	Musk mallow
Viper's bugloss	Wild carrot	Ox-eye daisy
Salad burnet	Yarrow	Meadow buttercup
Common vetch	Meadow cranesbill	
Cowslip	Goats' beard	
Sorrel	St. John's wort	
Yellow rattle		

Managing your meadow

- In dry weather water in the evening.
- Never cut shorter than 5-10 cm.
- Always remove cuttings to compost heap.
- Never add fertiliser or herbicide.
- A mown edge gives a tidier appearance.
- Never dig wild flowers from the countryside.
- Consider adding potted plants or seeds.
- Cut long grass (hay) with scythe or strimmer.
- Leave cut 'hay' for 2 days to allow seeds to fall.
- See 'Wildflowers in the Garden'
  in this series for details.

There are two main options which
will suit different wild flowers:

Spring meadow -
left to grow unchecked through the
spring but cut from July onwards.

Summer meadow -
left to grow from mid-June
but cut from October
onwards.

9

Flower border

Highly-bred, double-flowered plants generally have little pollen or nectar and rarely set seed, so they offer little to foraging insects or birds. However, the lists of both traditional cottage garden plants and wild flowers that are suitable for the borders of a bird garden could be much longer than those below. Try to choose some early and some late-flowering plants so that the wildlife larder is never bare. Both lists are in approximate order of flowering, though note that some species such as the dead-nettles and campions may flower almost all year round. Flowering periods of individual plants can also be extended by removing dead flower heads, but leave them in situ towards the end of the season to set seed. Before purchasing, check that they will grow in your soil type, though most will grow happily in a range of soils. Use a soil testing kit if you are unsure.

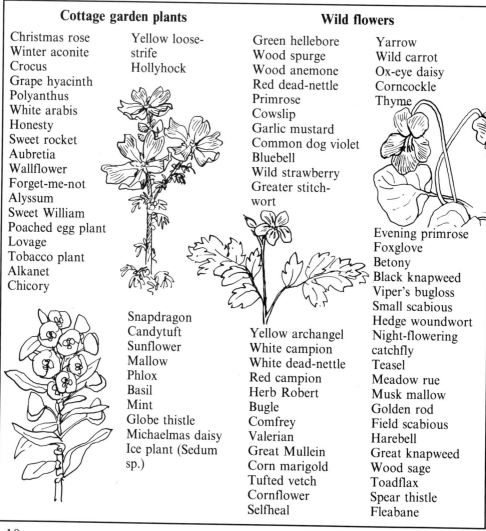

Cottage garden plants		Wild flowers	
Christmas rose	Yellow loose-	Green hellebore	Yarrow
Winter aconite	strife	Wood spurge	Wild carrot
Crocus	Hollyhock	Wood anemone	Ox-eye daisy
Grape hyacinth		Red dead-nettle	Corncockle
Polyanthus		Primrose	Thyme
White arabis		Cowslip	
Honesty		Garlic mustard	
Sweet rocket		Common dog violet	
Aubretia		Bluebell	
Wallflower		Wild strawberry	
Forget-me-not		Greater stitch-	
Alyssum		wort	
Sweet William			
Poached egg plant			Evening primrose
Lovage			Foxglove
Tobacco plant			Betony
Alkanet			Black knapweed
Chicory			Viper's bugloss
			Small scabious
	Snapdragon		Hedge woundwort
	Candytuft	Yellow archangel	Night-flowering
	Sunflower	White campion	catchfly
	Mallow	White dead-nettle	Teasel
	Phlox	Red campion	Meadow rue
	Basil	Herb Robert	Musk mallow
	Mint	Bugle	Golden rod
	Globe thistle	Comfrey	Field scabious
	Michaelmas daisy	Valerian	Harebell
	Ice plant (Sedum	Great Mullein	Great knapweed
	sp.)	Corn marigold	Wood sage
		Tufted vetch	Toadflax
		Cornflower	Spear thistle
		Selfheal	Fleabane

Climbers

A bare wall or fence can be transformed by climbing plants, and some climbers will also trail over hedges, pergolas and old tree stumps to good effect.
Mount any supporting trellis or netting on wooden blocks, say 5 cm. away from the wall. A sheltered micro-habitat then develops which is ideal for resting snails and butterflies and nesting or roosting birds.

Pyracantha deserves special mention for its berries and its remarkable tolerance of shade (e.g. on the north-facing side of the house). Ivy provides cover in summer for nesting birds, cover in winter for hibernating butterflies and at night for roosting birds, nectar for late autumn insects and fruit at the end of winter for the woodpigeons. Honeysuckle is also excellent, especially the native one since this gives not only a beautiful display of nectar-filled flowers which attract hordes of insects both in the day and at night, but also a good crop of autumn berries. Even the flaking strips of honeysuckle bark are popular with a range of birds for nesting material. A thornless variety of blackberry will give you and the birds a good painless feed. Leave the shrivelled late autumn berries for bullfinches.

Garden climbers and wall coverers

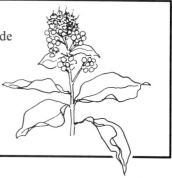

Pyracantha	Woody nightshade
Wisteria	Black bryony
Mahonia	White bryony
Cotoneaster	Blackberry
Vines	Ivy
Clematis	Honeysuckle

Pond and marsh plants

Certain plants quickly overrun a small pond. Avoid Canadian pondweed, various foreign water lilies, lesser spearwort, greater reedmace and common reed.
Even less vigorous plants may need thinning out each autumn. Include some from each category below to ensure the whole pond habitat is fully utilised.
Only native species suitable for a smaller pond are listed.

totally submerged	marginal/emergent	marsh (cont'd)
Water starwort	Bogbean	Meadowsweet
Hornwort	Flowering rush	Ragged robin
Water millfoil	Burr-reed	Meadow buttercup
Curled pondweed	Water mint	Cuckoo flower
	Water forget-me-not	Water avens
floating leaved	Brooklime	Gipsywort
Fringed water lily	Water plantain	Marsh marigold
Broad-leaved pond weed	Yellow flag	Marsh thistle
Amphibious bistort		Creeping Jenny
Water crowfoot	**marsh**	Bugle
	Purple loosestrife	Marsh woundwort
	Hemp agrimony	

Planning the garden

Carefully-prepared plans will help you make the most of a garden for all its inhabitants. Start by preparing a list of desirable features, bearing in mind especially such essentials as drying the washing, parking the car, reaching the shed and bird table in winter and being able to see the more interesting parts of the garden. This last point is one of the most important; think where you will sit to enjoy your garden and make this an integral part of the plan.

Measure the garden using a tape or piece of string knotted at metre intervals, and plot the shape on graph paper. Non-rectangular shapes are often best plotted by triangulation which, in brief, simply means that you should double check the shape by measuring diagonals as well as the length and breadth. Mark on existing features, both permanent (e.g. large tree) and potentially movable (e.g. shed). Note where the shade falls at key times of day (e.g. picnic lunch time) and any desirable or undesirable sightlines. Keep this 'before' layout as a master and use tracing paper to sketch a variety of possible 'after' layouts. Use cut-out scale shapes of features which have a fairly predictable size such as the shed, garden table and chairs, rotary washing line, swing and sandpit.

Then mark out your preferred design in the garden using stakes and string. Leave it for several days so that adjustments can be made before you finally start gardening.

Garden layout before

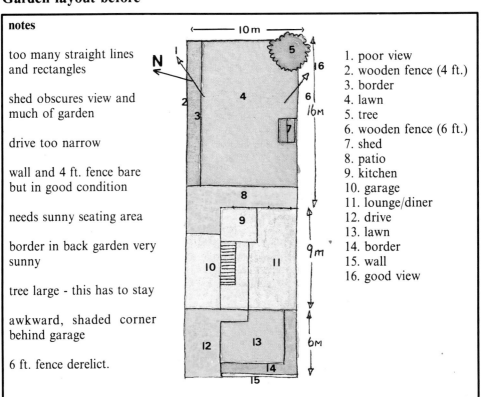

notes

too many straight lines and rectangles

shed obscures view and much of garden

drive too narrow

wall and 4 ft. fence bare but in good condition

needs sunny seating area

border in back garden very sunny

tree large - this has to stay

awkward, shaded corner behind garage

6 ft. fence derelict.

1. poor view
2. wooden fence (4 ft.)
3. border
4. lawn
5. tree
6. wooden fence (6 ft.)
7. shed
8. patio
9. kitchen
10. garage
11. lounge/diner
12. drive
13. lawn
14. border
15. wall
16. good view

12

Check list (example)
Essential lawn, garden bench, patio, paths, bird table, bird bath, swing, sandpit, compost heaps, shrubs, flower borders, nest boxes, shed, hedge, washing line
Desirable meadow, pond, trees, herb garden, rockery, fruit trees, vegetables, greenhouse, barbecue

Garden layout after

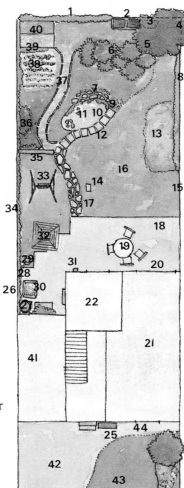

1. hedge
2. compost
3. prunings
4. tree retained
5. tunnel effect
6. shrubbery
7. rockery
8. mixed hedge
9. marsh
10. shallow for birds
11. pond
12. stone slabs/path
13. spring meadow
14. bird feeding station
15. new 4ft fence
16. open lawn
17. brick or crazy-paved path
18. extended patio
19. seating
20. window view points
21. lounge diner
22. kitchen
23. flower border
24. wall with shrubs over
25. trough/tub for climber
26. Pyracanthas
27. water butt
28. overflow to bird bath
29. bird bath over sump
30. sandpit
31. tit nest box
32. rotary drier next to patio
33. swing
34. climbers over fence
35. low stone wall
36. butterfly plants
37. log lined wood-chip path
38. vegetables and soft fruit
39. climber
40. shed
41. garage
42. hard standing for car
43. lawn
44. postman walkway

Trees, shrubs and hedgerow

As noted on page 6, native trees and shrubs attract more insects than introduced species. Although a mixed native woodland-edge effect is probably the best bird habitat you can develop in a garden, some cultivated species do have phenomenal crops of berries which many birds relish. Evergreens also provide much-needed shelter in winter; even the non-native cypress trees which abound in gardens are useful as night-time roost sites. Those which climb well or have dense growths of thorny branches provide nest sites. Trees and shrubs are also useful for screening unsightly sheds, compost heaps, factories and houses. They form effective windbreaks, provide fruit to eat, welcome shade in summer, even good sites for tree houses and rope swings! Early-flowering plants from the list on page 10 will grow happily beneath trees and shrubs before the shade becomes too dense.

Trees

In a large garden, do consider some specimen trees. Most broad-leaved trees will coppice well (simply cut them back to the ground when they become too large), but don't plant too close to the house or the roots may damage foundations. Plant fruit trees too, remembering of course to share the fruit! Crab apples are ideal since the fruit doesn't all ripen at the same time.

Recommended trees:

Any garden		Large garden	
Rowan .	Silver birch	English oak	Wild cherry
Whitebeam	Downy birch	Sessile oak	Small-leaved lime
Wild service tree	Pussy willow	Beech	Scots pine
Bird cherry	Field maple	Ash	Larch
Hawthorn	Aspen	White willow	
Crab apple	'Cypress' species	Hornbeam	
Alder			

Dead wood

Dead wood supports ten times as many species of wildlife (fungi, beetles, woodlice etc.) as live wood, so don't tidy up too much! Stack prunings where they can rot down. Don't put dead leaves and grass cuttings in the dustbin; pile them on the compost heap. Recycle as much garden waste as possible with the aid of nature's dustmen.

Shrubs

For cultivated berry-bearing shrubs, you can't beat pyracantha and the various varieties of berberis and cotoneaster. The buddleias are good nectar sources, as are hebes, lavender and rosemary.

Suitable native shrubs

Wild privet	Hazel	Dogwood	Hawthorn
Dog rose	Elder	Wayfaring tree	Holly *(Note that*
Blackthorn	Purging buckthorn	Guelder rose	*only the female hol-*
Yew	Alder buckthorn	Spindle	*ly has berries, and*
			only if a male grows
			nearby.)

Hedgerow

For a good, thick, easily-maintained
hedge, use hawthorn as the main component,
plus perhaps 20-25% of two or three from
the list below. Wildlife-rich hedges are
best cut to an A shape very early
in each spring, so that sunlight
reaches lower branches
and so birds are
not deprived of
winter food.
They make wonderful
'corridors' down
which animals
and birds
will travel.

Hedgerow shrubs

Dogwood	Hazel
Holly	Guelder rose
Field maple	Dog rose
Beech	Hornbeam
Wild privet	Blackthorn

Some Resident Birds: Making them feel at home

These birds can be attracted to gardens all year round, by providing suitable habitats, natural and artificial foods and a range of nest sites. Those marked * will all, at least occasionally, use 'tailor-made' nest boxes (see page 42).

Treecreeper*
Needs mature trees; smear porridge or mixture of fat, crushed nuts and bread crumbs, into rough bark.

Nuthatch*
Mature trees and fat as for treecreeper, but also nuts, seeds (including melon), cake, cheese and bread.

Long-tailed Tit
When icy takes scraps of meat, bread and cheese, also smeared fat. In March provide fluffy feathers for nest - in prickly bush.

Pied Wagtail*
Prefers open areas. In hard weather put tiny crumbs in short grass or on paved areas.

Great Spotted Woodpecker*
Likes nuts, suet, oats etc. in container over 20m from house and fixed to tree trunk.

16

Robin*
Many artificial foods; fond of mealworms and earthworms. Old kettles amongst thick ivy good for nesting.

Mistle Thrush
Takes kitchen scraps and windfall apples in snow, but prefers berries of yew, holly, rowan and hawthorn, especially away from house.

Blue Tit*
The small-hole nest box inhabitant. Fond of peanuts, suet, fat, coconut and cheese.

Goldcrest
Welcomes conifers. Takes crumbs, fat and grated cheese in hard weather.

Wren
Tangles of undergrowth, wood piles, cracks and crevices ideal. Sprinkle grated cheese beneath bushes in winter.

Greenfinch
Relishes peanuts, wheat and sunflower seeds in winter. Leave sunflower plants in situ or save seed heads for wintry days.

Goldfinch
Eats small seeds at table, also seeds from teasel, thistle and burdock.

17

Some Summer Visitors: Improving their breeding success

A range of birds, mostly insect-eating species, migrate from Africa and southern Europe to raise families in British gardens. - Those marked * will take to specially-designed nest boxes (see pages 44 - 46).

Blackcap
*Trees and shrubs essential.
Some overwinter and come for bird bath,
 berries (e.g. ivy), kitchen scraps,
fat, seeds, dried fruit and even peanuts.*

Willow Warbler
*Likes shrubs and trees,
especially sallow in spring.
Nests near ground in cover.*

Swift*
*Nests in colonies
within eaves of houses
but collects all food and
nesting material in flight*

Spotted Flycatcher*
*Flies from fences etc.
to catch insects.
Nests against wall or
trunk, on a ledge or
amongst climbing plants.*

Swallow*
*Nests on and/or against walls,
rafters, beams and joists inside
garages, porches and outhouses.
May take wet mud from tray
in the open for nest.*

House Martin*
*Like swallow, feeds on the wing
and may take wet mud.
Nests beneath eaves of houses.*

Plants eaten by immature stages of insects

When laying their eggs, adult insects often search for particular plants, usually native species. Their larvae or nymphs are often very specific in their requirements; sometimes they will only feed on a single plant species.

Listed below is a selection of plants to which the more common moths and butterflies will be attracted. Over 300 moth species may be found even in an 'average' garden, so the moth list is necessarily selective.

Moths

Green Oak Tortrix, Leopard Moth, Black Arches, Peppered Moth, Mottled, Willow and Brindled Beauty, Buff-tip, Coxcomb Prominent, Winter Moth, Early and Feathered Thorn, Swallowtail, March Moth, Common Quaker, Common Footman, Dunbar, Grey Dagger.	These moths will feed on a variety of trees and shrubs, e.g.) Oak, Lime, Poplar, Hawthorn, Blackthorn, Sallow, Elm, Ivy Birch, Privet, Lilac, Plum, Cherry, Apple, Rose etc.
Herald, Swallow Prominent, Puss Moth, Sallow Kitten, Poplar Hawkmoth, Red Underwing.	These moths are examples of those which use a more restricted range of trees: Poplar, Sallow, Willow and Aspen
Angle Shades, Shuttle-shaped Dart, Garden Tiger, Hebrew Character, Large Yellow Underwing, Flame, White and Buff Ermine, Muslin Moth, Bright-line Brown-eye.	Many moths take a selection of low-growing plants such as Dandelion, Docks, Plantain, Dead-nettles, Chickweed and Knotgrass
Dark Arches, Common Wainscot, Common Rustic, Drinker Moth, the various 'grass moths'.	These moths specialise in grasses such as Couch, Cocksfoot and Meadow Grasses

Many moths will feed on cultivated garden plants (as well as more natural food plants) e.g.

Garden Carpet	Cabbage family
Magpie Moth	Currants and Gooseberry
Deaths Head Hawkmoth	Potato, Snowberry and Jasmine
Privet Hawkmoth	Lilac and Viburnum
Elephant Hawkmoth	Fucshia

Butterflies

Red Admiral, Small Tortoiseshell, Peacock, Comma, Painted Lady	Stinging Nettle
Small Copper	Docks and Sorrels
Brimstone	Alder Buckthorn, Purging Buckthorn
Large White, Small White	Cabbage family, Nasturtium
Orange Tip	Hedge Mustard, Honesty, Cuckoo Flower, Sweet Rocket
Comma, Red Admiral	Hop
Painted Lady	Thistles
Comma	Sallow, Elm
Common Blue	Birdsfoot Trefoil, Tormentil, Red Clover, Rest Harrow
Purple Hairstreak	Oak
Green-veined White, Orange Tip	Charlock and Garlic Mustard
Holly Blue	Dogwood, Holly, Ivy
Meadow Brown, Wall Brown, Small Heath, Gatekeeper, Ringlet, Speckled Wood, Large, Essex and Small Skippers.	Various grasses, e.g. Yorkshire Fog, Couch, Fescues, Cocksfoot and Meadow grasses (not Rye Grass)

Making a pond

An ideal pond has some water only 2-4 cm deep in which birds can bathe. A steep-sided pond surrounded by overhanging stone slabs is of little use (though a strategically placed stick will help), and may result in some birds (and hedgehogs) drowning. Even frogs prefer a gently-shelving bank to climb up after finishing breeding.

water - from the mains is acceptable; from the roof (not recently felted) is better since this will have less nutrients and the resulting initial flush of green slime will be less pronounced. Allow to settle for a few days before planting; animals will arrive with pond plants, or by flying, though a bucketful of water from a nearby garden pond may speed up the process.

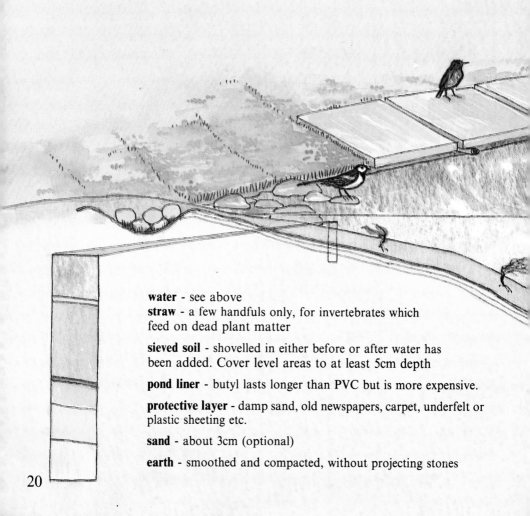

water - see above

straw - a few handfuls only, for invertebrates which feed on dead plant matter

sieved soil - shovelled in either before or after water has been added. Cover level areas to at least 5cm depth

pond liner - butyl lasts longer than PVC but is more expensive.

protective layer - damp sand, old newspapers, carpet, underfelt or plastic sheeting etc.

sand - about 3cm (optional)

earth - smoothed and compacted, without projecting stones

20

depth - 60-100 cm is ideal. Shallower ponds may freeze solid, killing fish and other animals

shelves - at about 25cm depth, for plants

trench with stones - about 20cm deep, to keep the edge of the liner buried

marsh area - lined trench with soil but open to the water, liner 'holed' to give poor drainage effect. Good bird feeding area

paving stones - provide easy access for people and birds; slope slightly away from pond for safety

overflow pipe - to soakaway pit; cover pond end of pipe with wire mesh and keep clean

turves - saved from the digging phase

plants - introduce in May or June if possible, either directly in the soil, or in plant baskets; see page 11 for species

waterfall - running water and a series of pools provide an attractive range of drinking and bathing locations for birds

rockery - use spoil from pond. Crevices between rocks are excellent mini-beast haunts

One of the most important ingredients of the bird garden recipe is water. Of course, without water no plants can grow and we have already established how important they are. In times of drought, water thoroughly and infrequently, rather than little and often, preferably in the evening when evaporation is less. Try to siphon water from your own bath through a hose, out through a window and into a large water butt or two, perhaps via the roof/gutter which normally feeds the butt. This will generate a most welcome supply of water when hose-pipe bans are in force.

Birds that feed on moist caterpillars may need very little drinking water and nestling birds are, by definition, unable to leave the nest to drink. However, many others drink regularly, especially seed-eating species like sparrows and finches, and especially during hot weather.

All birds need to bathe and some have developed the unlikely-sounding but apparently no less effective methods of bathing in dust and even smoke instead of water. Whatever the method, the aim is to rid feathers of dirt and parasites. A good preen always follows and waterproofing oil from a gland just above the tail completes the process. Given sufficient food, the bird can survive the coldest, wettest and windiest weather. **Indeed, fresh water is probably most important to birds during freezing weather when the protective functions of feathers are tested to the limit. Extra effort on our part at these times may make the difference between life and death for the birds in our garden.**

Bird baths

Bird baths double as drinking places and come in all shapes, sizes and prices.
Almost any container will do: an old dish, plant pot saucer, dustbin lid supported by three bricks etc. Provide at least one gently-shelving side for small birds, or place a rough stone in the middle.

Bird baths can become rather messy so a periodic scrub with a stiff-bristled brush is recommended. If convenient, route the water butt overflow pipe into the bird bath, preferably with a drainage sump beneath. This helps to keep it topped up and rinsed through. However, keep siphoned soapy bath water out of the bird bath, as it might affect the birds' waterproofing oil.

Keep bird baths away from bushes where cats hide, and remember that your own enjoyment will be greatly increased if you can sit or stand (e.g. doing the washing up!) in comfort and watch the birds as they bathe.

Never add anti-freeze or salt to bird-bath water. A metal dustbin lid bath can be kept free of ice by putting a slow burning nightlight candle beneath, but an appropriately-wired aquarium heater and thermostat, covered by stones, is best. The standard alternative is the morning kettle of hot water!

Finally, look for interesting behaviour where birds and water are concerned.
Wrens bathe in dew, crows and magpies dunk dry bread in water, and sparrows perch very upright in rain so as not to get too wet. Watch how only pigeons suck water up as we do; other species take only a beakful at a time.

The pond

A well-designed garden pond will guarantee hours of good bird watching each year. It will act both as a giant bird bath and as a rich source of other wildlife. Many insects such as water beetles and assorted bugs (water boatmen, water scorpion etc.) live within water throughout their lives. Many others, including mayflies, caddisflies, midges (most of which do not bite) and the large and dramatic dragonflies emerge into the air as adults having spent their earlier stages in the water.

Goldfish might attract a kingfisher (if you are lucky) or a heron, but are generally not welcome in a wildlife pond since they eat many animals which would otherwise become food for birds. If you must have fish try sticklebacks which will not dominate the pond, or consider having two ponds, one with fish and one without.

If you are really keen, go for two ponds, a waterfall, a fountain and separate bird baths. Rather like the modern swimming pool with water chute, wave machine and baby pool, this should attract birds of all dispositions! Do make sure any electrical equipment is installed professionally and erect a fence to keep small children safe if necessary.

There are some excellent books on making different kinds of ponds, including one in this series 'Starting a Wildlife Pond'. The diagram on pages 20 and 21 shows the basic construction of a pond made with a flexible liner. This is one of the simplest, most versatile and successful methods.

Recommended plants are listed on page 11.

Even a small garden can accommodate some of th

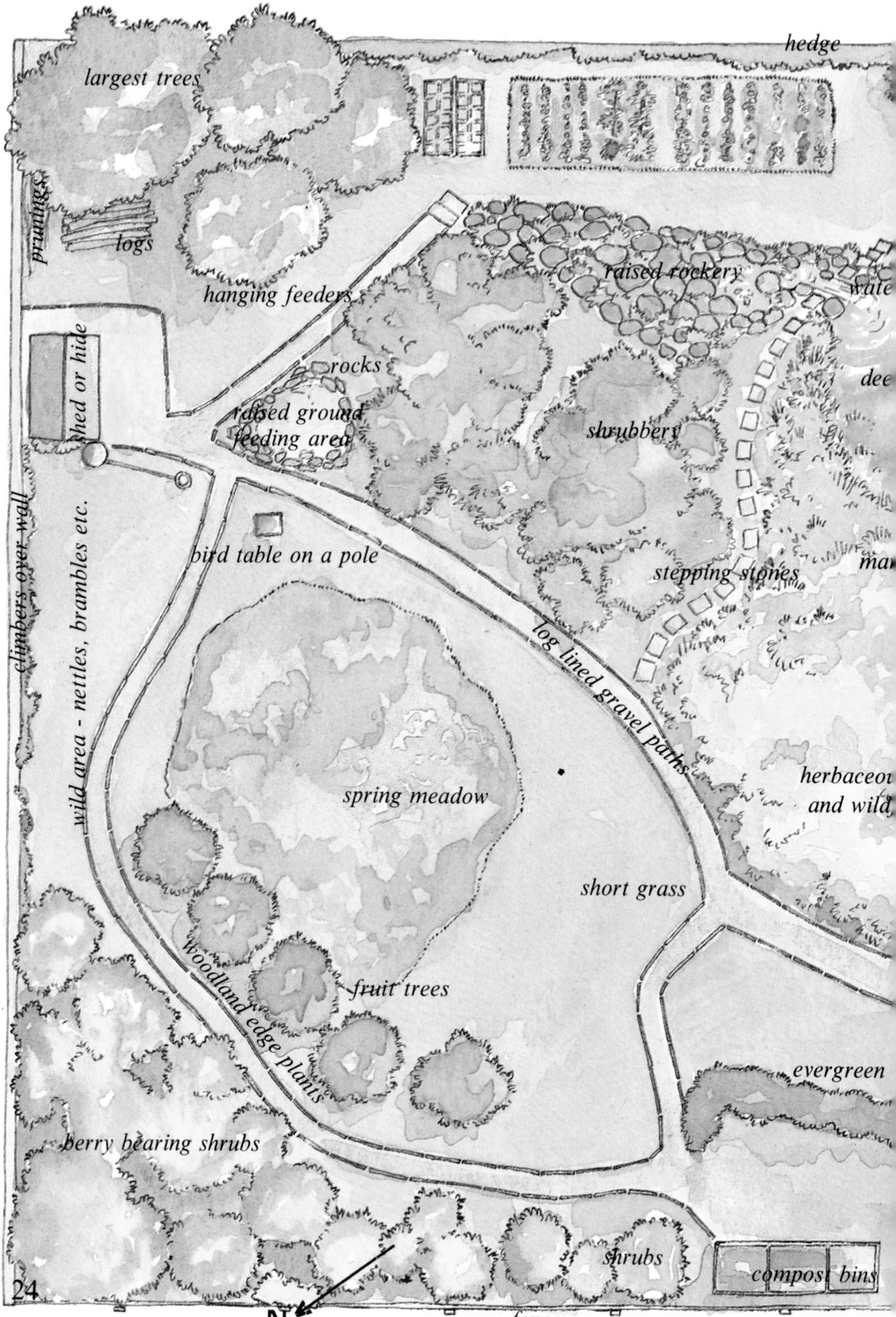

hedge

largest trees

logs

pruning

hanging feeders

raised rockery

wate

rocks

dee

shed or hide

raised ground feeding area

shrubbery

bird table on a pole

stepping stones

ma

climbers over wall

wild area – nettles, brambles etc.

log lined gravel paths

spring meadow

herbaceo and wild

short grass

Woodland edge plants

fruit trees

evergreen

berry bearing shrubs

24

shrubs

compost bins

N

fence

ures.

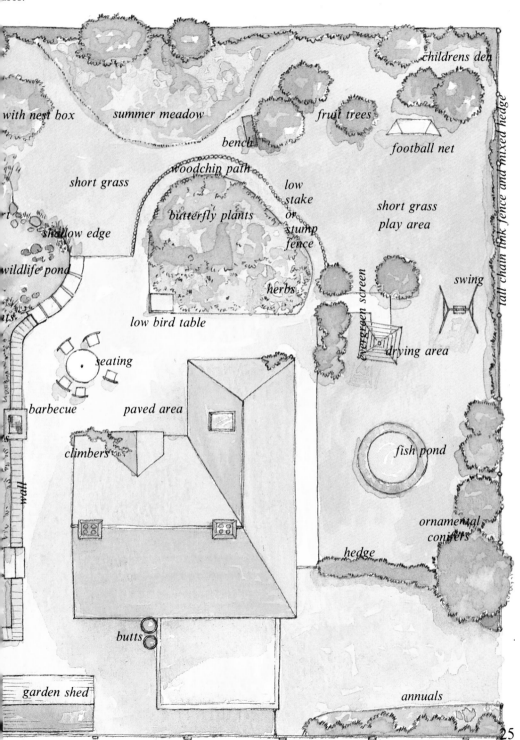

with nest box

summer meadow

childrens den

fruit trees

bench

football net

woodchip path

short grass

low
stake
or
stump
fence

butterfly plants

short grass
play area

shallow edge

herbs

swing

wildlife pond

low bird table

evergreen screen

drying area

seating

barbecue

paved area

climbers

fish pond

wall

ornamental
conifers

butts

hedge

garden shed

annuals

tall chain link fence and mixed hedge

25

There is a wide selection of mini-habitats and other 'little extras' which, at least for some bird species at certain times of year, might well make all the difference.

Compost heap

Every garden should have a conveniently-located compost heap, or preferably two, one maturing and one being filled up. All vegetation, dead or alive, is food for something else, so it follows that grass cuttings, autumn leaves, unwanted weeds, potato peelings, apple cores, cabbage leaves and a host of other household and garden 'waste' should be recycled. The most obvious benefit is the supply of nutrient-rich compost for the vegetable patch and flower border, but the frost-free decomposing heap itself is wonderful for worms, tiny creepy crawlies and microscopic fungi and bacteria.

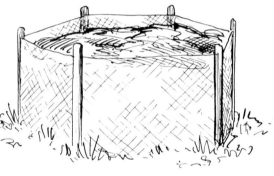

Not only will birds dig out the animal inhabitants, but a toad, hedgehog, slow-worm or grass snake may also take up residence. These do no harm and help to keep slugs and snails under control.

Whether a purpose-bought, slatted timber compost heap or a D.I.Y. stake and wire mesh version, the main considera-tion is air circulation; the animals aiding the process of decomposition must be able to breathe. Place it directly on earth or raised on a platform of bricks, perhaps covered with a layer of sticks. In many circumstances, leaf mould is a good substitute for peat, and those with both space and a good supply of leaves will do themselves and the dwindling peat bogs a favour by reserving one heap solely for leaves.

Other heaps

All too often 'unwanted' logs, planks of wood, seed trays, bricks, stones and prunings are thrown into the dustbin, burnt or taken to the local council tip.

If you can, allocate spaces in which to pile these; it can be done very neatly, especially if the piles are kept only for a single type of 'rubbish'. As with the compost heap, a large number of mini-beasts will quickly move in and provide (i.e. become!) food for a variety of bird species through the year.

Robins and wrens might even take up residence and build a nest.

With a little imagination, many salvaged items can serve a dual purpose. Large, flat-topped sections of tree trunks make excellent stepping 'stones' and bird bath pedestals. Logs, rocks and bricks can define edges of paths, hold back raised earth banks or be made into a double wall infilled with earth and covered with climbing plants.

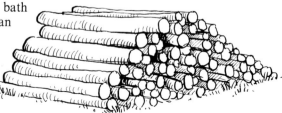

In most situations vegetation grows up through piles and disguises them very effectively. This also provides shade from the hot sun in summer. It is worth incorporating a dish of some kind or even an old plastic sack to catch and retain rainwater. The increased humidity may well attract frogs to shelter there.

Dust bath

Some birds, especially sparrows whose ancestors lived in dry, desert conditions, flap and wriggle in dry, dusty earth until literally covered in dust.
Perhaps surprisingly, this rids feathers of animal parasites and oily dirt.

To make a dust bath, try regularly raking a corner of the flower bed, or put out a tray of dry sand or dusty earth where it won't matter if the contents get flapped out! Drainage holes in the tray will let the rain out and thus help to keep it dry.

Stone anvil

Especially in dry weather, song thrushes eat many garden snails since worms burrow deeper into the soil when the ground becomes hard and dry. To crack open a snail shell the thrush holds it by the rim and bashes it against a stone or some other hard surface. If you have a patio or rockery which is not too near the house, this will be more than adequate as an anvil, if not, then do consider providing a slab of stone somewhere mutually convenient.

Grit

Finches and sparrows swallow small pieces of grit which lodge in their gizzards. Here, any seeds eaten are ground down before passing into the stomach.
Try providing a small tray of grit, swept from the road side and washed, and watch to see if any is taken.

Nettle patch

Stinging nettles are extremely valuable for wildlife. Not only do the caterpillars of some of our most attractive butterflies rely solely on nettles for their food, but studies have shown that many other insects also depend on them... and as usual, the birds are quick to learn.

To stop nettles spreading, grow them in a tub or bath, surround them with a square of stone paving slabs or mow adjacent grass. Cut the plants in rotation every few weeks to ensure a constant supply of fresh, succulent leaves.
Any with batches of caterpillars should obviously be left, and in autumn leave some to set seed for the birds to eat.

The same patch could house other tall 'weeds' such as rose bay willow-herb (food plant of the elephant hawk-moth), sowthistle and teasel (both enjoyed by goldfinches). So long as it is kept under control, such a wild patch is an asset to the bird garden.

song thrush

Prominent perch

Many birds like to proclaim their territories by singing from a perch which affords a good view of the garden. Often this might be the roof or chimneypot of the house itself, but garden sheds, trees, fences and almost any other prominent lookout may suffice. A tall cane, bean pole or washing-line post may quickly be adopted if alternatives are scarce.

Do try to recognise birds by their songs and calls, as this adds a new dimension to identification and your own enjoyment.

28

Food from a tree

A mature tree feeds a huge variety of wildlife both amongst its branches and further afield. It provides nesting and roosting sites, song and lookout posts, and branches from which bird feeders can be hung or to which nest boxes can be attached. In its shade the woodland floor environment is ideal for many wild flowers and the wildlife they attract.

This illustration shows some selected and simplified food chains starting with the various parts of an oak tree.

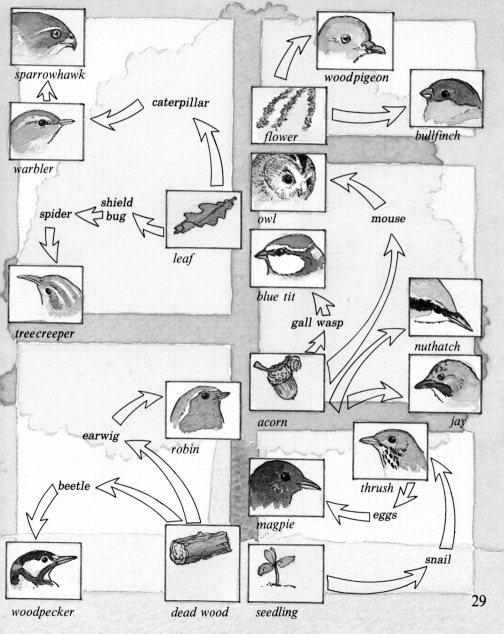

sparrowhawk

caterpillar

woodpigeon

warbler

flower

bullfinch

spider

shield bug

leaf

owl

mouse

blue tit

gall wasp

nuthatch

treecreeper

earwig

robin

acorn

jay

beetle

thrush

magpie

eggs

woodpecker

dead wood

seedling

snail

Advice on how to plant a tree, watering, propagation and so on is contained in many gardening books so, instead, some rather unorthodox tips are offered here which are more specific to those intending to garden for birds.

Pests in the garden? ... give up!

Many a would-be bird-friendly gardener fears that the wildlife might get out of control. Apart from direct damage by birds, people worry that all the wild flowers (weeds!), dead leaves and log piles could breed a plague of slugs in the vegetables, aphids on the beans and codlin moth maggots in the fruit!

However, such problems rarely occur in a good wildlife garden simply because the same conditions favour a host of predators. A hedgehog consumes some 70g of slugs, beetles, caterpillars and other invertebrates every night. A pair of blue tits find perhaps 500 caterpillars a day to feed their young. Hoverfly larvae, lacewings and ladybirds all eat aphids. Even the much-maligned wasp collects insects one by one for its larvae. We should encourage these predators, not exterminate their prey with chemicals that might also kill the predators themselves. Insecticide sprays and slug pellets have no place in the ideal bird garden; these and very carefully applied herbicides and fungicides should only be used as a last resort. The RSPB have useful guidelines on chemicals in the garden.

Happily, organic gardening is an expanding pastime, and it really is worth both reading up on the subject (try the Henry Doubleday Research Association for a start) and experimenting yourself. Regular planned crop rotation prevents pests building up. Mixed planting, e.g. leeks next to carrots, similarly controls some undesirables. Wild or cultivated flowers, marigolds for example, planted amongst vegetables, seem both to kill off pests and attract their predators.

The most oft-quoted 'wildlife-friendly' way of killing slugs is a sunken cup of beer. Cover this with a flat, slightly-raised stone or plank of wood to keep hedgehogs out. Hollowed-out half oranges and grapefruits are also popular, and an evening stroll with a torch will yield a good catch simply picked off the ground to be carried off to neighbouring woodland.

Having said all this **the best tip for anyone with a pest problem may be to give up!** Give up, that is, trying to do something about the pests. Don't grow difficult plants, or if you must, grow them somewhere safe. Be content to let nature find its own balance, and learn to enjoy life as it is rather than impose your own inevitably unnatural designs.

Children in the garden? ... join them!

Too few children have a real love of nature. Increasingly, society is breeding people who are more at home in neon-lit, computer-powered concrete jungles like London than in sunlit, chlorophyll-powered countryside. Take time to enjoy your garden with children: the swings, sandpit, football ... flowers, insects and birds. **Encourage them to appreciate wildlife in all its beauty and to accept that each worm, ant, wasp and sparrow has a right to live and a role to play in the complex web of life.**

Be positive: give them a portion of the garden to manage, explain that ants do us no harm, show them how to rescue a daddy-longlegs or spider from the lounge without loss of life or limb, help them make a nest box of their own, listen to their accounts of new discoveries and praise them for every achievement.

Then perhaps their children will have wildlife to appreciate too.

Birds in the garden? ... watch out!

Creating a garden for birds is of genuine conservation value; if all the million or so acres of gardens in Britain were managed for wildlife, our living environment would indeed be rich. However, **your own personal enjoyment and sense of fulfilment will be much increased if you allocate time to watching the birds.** Watch for detail, signs of intelligence, partnerships, confrontations and much more.

Most species have tell-tale features which indicate their age, sex, breeding condition and so on. Thus a young dunnock has dull, mud-coloured eyes, which gradually become rich chestnut by the next spring. A male starling in breeding plumage has a blue base to his bill; the female's is pink (an easy one to remember!). A male blackbird has dark brown wings until its second autumn moult. The real challenge lies in the fact that birds recognise each other individually just as people recognise each other. Picking out the odd bird with a few albino feathers is easy, but how many of your other garden birds do you really know?

As you watch birds and ask yourself questions about them, you will soon discover how well they are adapted to garden life. How soon do birds find food on the bird table? How quickly do different species master a new feeder or kind of food? Do they watch each other? Do any birds hoard food, and then come back for it?

A bird succeeds in life only when it raises young bearing its own genetic make-up, and this is possible only through breeding partnerships and, in crowded garden habitats, territorial confrontations. Thus, although the female blue tit builds the nest, lays the eggs and incubates them, her mate proclaims and defends a territory large enough for the whole family, and for ages for them both. Despite apparent constant quarrelling, starlings do benefit from feeding together in a tight flock; there are more eyes to watch for the local sparrowhawk for a start. The more timid species do have to wait their turn for food at a bird table, yet even these survive by foraging in different ways, at different times and in different parts of the garden.

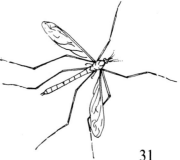

31

Backyard oasis

The illustration shows how even a shaded backyard can become a haven for birds and other wildlife.

Making full use of height is one of the secrets. Notice the following features:

- tit box high on house wall, by window
  - bird table within arm's reach, by window
    - pyracantha and ivy trained up wall and fence
      - food scattered on the ground or a board
        - raised flower bed, surrounded by logs or bricks - this doubles as a garden seat
          - bird bath resting on a thick stump
            - buddleia in a corner
              - a small pond

The view from the window
This is really important. Decide what you want to see and what needs to be screened. Imagine how the garden will look from **inside** the house. You'll probably spend as much time looking at your garden as being in it.

Whilst people generally live in a protected society where the sick are cared for, the hungry are fed and the life of even the oldest is prolonged as far as is possible, birds live in a world where only the fittest survive. **The simple fact is that every year, on average, as many birds die as are born.** This applies to any species in any habitat, unless the population of breeding birds is to increase or decrease. We need not be too concerned at the sight of a dead bird or when a well-known feathered friend suddenly 'disappears' from the garden.

A typical pair of blue tits might lay eleven eggs (even fourteen or fifteen are possible), and ten of these might hatch. If both adults and all the nestlings survived, a total of six pairs would live the following year in the same area which previously supported only one pair! Clearly this would be impossible; for long-term population stability only two of the family should live to breed successfully the next year. On average the survivors are one of the adults (about 50% of full-grown blue tits die each year), and one of the youngsters (about 10% survival in their first year).

Over-production of young, followed by heavy mortality, ensures that only fit birds perpetuate the species. If the population of a species does fall (e.g. because of unusually bad winter weather), a swift recovery often occurs since competition between remaining individuals for food and good nest sites is reduced and over 50% (and 10%) survive.

Each young bird, once it has 'flown the nest', is on its own. Each might still learn from other birds and even benefit from their presence in the garden, but the most successful are the vigilant, opportunistic, dominant individuals who lay claim to the best territories.

Birds as pests

The principle of over-production and mortality applies to both animals and plants. An oak tree may produce millions of acorns during its life-time but even if only one of these survives to maturity, it has succeeded. A pear or apple tree produces very many more flowers each spring than it could possibly 'allow' to yield fruit in the autumn.

It follows that the sparrowhawk which catches birds at a bird table, the bullfinch which eats the buds from the fruit tree, and the magpie which raids nests in the garden, are simply part of the natural thinning-out process. We can welcome almost any wild bird into our garden; it should fit in without upsetting the overall natural balance to any great extent.

For those who have a genuine and serious bird pest problem, the best advice is probably to physically exclude birds from the problem area. Netting over currants or cabbages, a good covering of scaraweb over pear trees in winter, and even a wire 'cage' around a nest box threatened by crows, are all more likely to succeed than shooting, poisoning or scaring.

Cats and squirrels

Both these introduced mammals raid bird tables and nests, and of course cats also kill adult birds. Again, both can be accepted as 'natural' predators, but certain measures can be taken to reduce their effect. Try to site nest boxes out of reach, on the side of the house if necessary. Blue tits, the most common users of nest boxes, readily take to such inaccessible sites provided other conditions are suitable. A good tangle of barbed wire or brambles beneath a box may also deter cats.

Avoid the more rustic, easily-climbed bird tables, and if possible site the table some 2-3 metres away from cover so that cats cannot approach unseen.

Squirrels negotiate remarkably complex and difficult routes to bird tables, but they are not unbeatable. Protect a free-standing bird table by placing a smooth plastic drainpipe over the stake, followed by a large upturned biscuit tin, and then the table top. Squirrels are unable to grip the drainpipe sufficiently well to jump out and up to the table itself. A range of mostly rather expensive squirrel-proof feeders are also now available and certainly worth investing in to solve a severe squirrel problem.

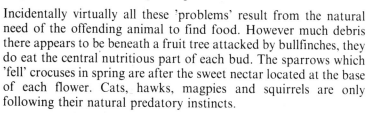

Incidentally virtually all these 'problems' result from the natural need of the offending animal to find food. However much debris there appears to be beneath a fruit tree attacked by bullfinches, they do eat the central nutritious part of each bud. The sparrows which 'fell' crocuses in spring are after the sweet nectar located at the base of each flower. Cats, hawks, magpies and squirrels are only following their natural predatory instincts.

First aid for birds

All birds, their nests and eggs are protected by law. It is also illegal to take wild birds into captivity. However, it is permitted to keep an injured bird if the sole purpose is to care for it and then release it as soon as it is fit again.

The key point is, don't attempt to care for any wild bird unless you have the necessary time, money, expertise and perseverance to bring it back to full health and strength. It is often best to take a suffering bird to a veterinary surgeon to be humanely destroyed. If in doubt, leave the bird where it is.

Temporary housing

Most birds stop struggling in the dark. Find a well-ventilated cardboard box with a secure lid before catching a bird. Line it with newspaper or absorbent kitchen paper and add a perch or two. For birds staying for several days, a budgerigar cage covered with a towel is ideal, or you could make a D.I.Y cage from a wooden box and some weldmesh.

Injured birds

A little basic first aid may enable a stunned bird or one with a small wound to recover. Treat surface cuts with mild antiseptic and water or a gentian-violet wound spray. Remove any tiny white sausage-shaped blow-fly eggs from the bird's nostrils, mouth, ears and under its tail. Keep it warm, and it may be ready for release after only an hour or so.

Orphans

Many a young thrush, blackbird or starling leaves its nest before it can fly properly, and most apparently-abandoned fledglings are simply waiting for their next feed - from their parents. If you find such a baby bird retire to a distance, so you don't frighten either the youngster or its parents. Only if it is not fed within two hours should you consider disturbing it further. Remember that you cannot hope to give it the attention it should normally receive; it may never learn basic survival techniques, such as flying away from a cat or dog!

Food

Fledglings need feeding at least hourly during daylight. For young birds try crushed soaked biscuit or moist baby cereal, a little scrambled egg or frag ments of raw mince, beef or chicken. Aphids are more natural, or try pieces of caterpillar or earthworm. Add a vitamin-mineral supplement as soon as possible. Older birds may take pet shop mixtures, grated cheese and tinned cat or dog food, and sparrows, finches and buntings eat seeds or crushed peanuts. Use blunt tweezers for dry food, but squirt wet mixtures into a bird's mouth from a plastic syringe with the tip cut off. Push food well into a young bird's throat as its parent would.

Early on the day of release, leave the bird in its cage outside for a few minutes before letting it fly. Provide food at this release point for several days while the bird becomes accustomed to its new-found and rightful freedom.

Food will attract more birds to your garden than anything else, and planning your garden restaurant or service station, furniture included, can be great fun. Whilst natural food has the best nutritional content and balance, many of the man-made 'artificial' alternatives are excellent. Indeed some species, like the pigeons in city centres, live very well almost solely on waste from people. Garden birds are highly skilled at finding suitable food in gardens, so don't worry too much about just what, where, when and how to provide food. Anything inappropriate will simply be left behind and you can move it onto the compost heap.

Even though natural foods are usually plentiful in summer and autumn, you can still enjoy feeding birds at these times if you want. Nestling tits may choke on whole peanuts brought by unwitting parents when the supply of caterpillars is low, so peanuts put out during May and June should be grated or placed in containers with a small-sized mesh through which the birds can remove only broken pieces. Avoid desiccated coconut and uncooked rice as they can swell up inside a bird with fatal results, and very spicy or salty foods are unsuitable (e.g salted peanuts).

In winter, even though you may see only a few birds at one time, your generosity may attract several hundred birds when natural foods run short. To ensure that a single magpie or flock of starlings do not quickly devour or carry off food put out for less assertive birds, pin or tie the food down, or shred, grate, mash, spread or otherwise de-lump and distribute the food. The larger birds find it difficult to manage fiddly or mushy food efficiently and may not look for scraps thrown beneath the bushes. Wire mesh will also exclude larger birds.

If you do enjoy feeding birds, ask the BTO about their Garden Bird Feeding Survey. Many ordinary people collect data throughout the country, as part of a complex and invaluable scientific study.

Bird tables

Birds do not appreciate good carpentry or rustic tables with thatched roofs.
However, it is worth spending time and effort (or money) on a bird table that is both durable and practical.

The most basic design is a wooden post topped by a flat board, perhaps 50 cm or more square, preferably partly edged with strips of wood to keep food on.
Many improvements and embellishments can be made. Wooden blocks or struts beneath the table top make it more secure; a roof keeps rain off and can house a seed hopper, and a selection of nails or cup hooks will support hanging feeders. The whole thing can be free standing on a movable base or permanently hammered into the ground; it can be six foot high or resting on the ground. The table top, with or without a roof, can be hung from a tree branch or wall-mounted bracket with chains or rope, or it can be modified to rest on a window sill. The choice is yours!

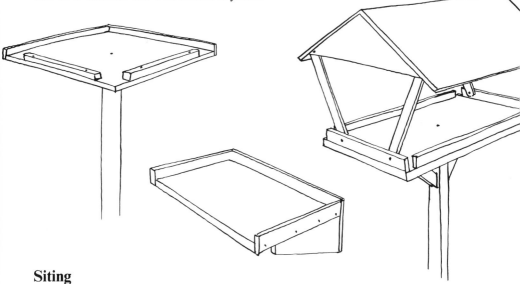

Siting

Position your bird table where you can see it easily without altering your daily routine.
The better the viewing, the greater your enjoyment and the more often you will bother to take out scraps of food on cold, wet and windy days when birds need them most.

The ideal position is about 2-3 m from a tree, too far for a cat or squirrel to jump (see also page 35) but close enough even for timid birds. Experiment with different locations. A table within a tree is usually popular with most species, one out in the open favours flocking birds like greenfinches, one adjacent to a house deters timid species but still attracts others (notably siskins). Feeders can even be hung in front of a window from a stick wedged between the surrounding brickwork. Don't forget that birds such as the dunnock, song thrush, chaffinch and reed bunting prefer to feed on the ground, so spread some seeds and small scraps on the grass or patio.

Wherever your bird table or feeding station is, it should need little maintenance except of course regular stocking with food and an occasional scrub with warm soapy water.

Feeders

Kitchen scraps can be simply dumped on a table to be quickly eaten or carried away, but purchased seed and peanuts are best placed in feeders of some kind.

There is a great variety of excellent feeders available from retailers or organisations specialising in wildlife gardening products, but they are not always cheap. Many of the more rustic feeders sold at garden centres have a small capacity and need refilling rather too often. It is definitely worth making your own from odd pieces of wood and wire mesh.

The 1/4 inch weld mesh used on commercial peanut containers is ideal, but it is not generally available. If necessary, buy one of the cylindrical mesh containers and re-use the mesh on two or three home-made feeders. Experiment with different designs: make one which allows access only from below for the tits, nuthatches and woodpeckers; make a large chip-basket-like one out of chicken wire into which you can drop the chicken carcass; make another with a hole rather like a nest box. Even upturned coffee jars with 6 mm holes drilled in the lid work quite well.

The main thing to remember is that there are no strict rules, do your own thing and watch how the birds adapt.

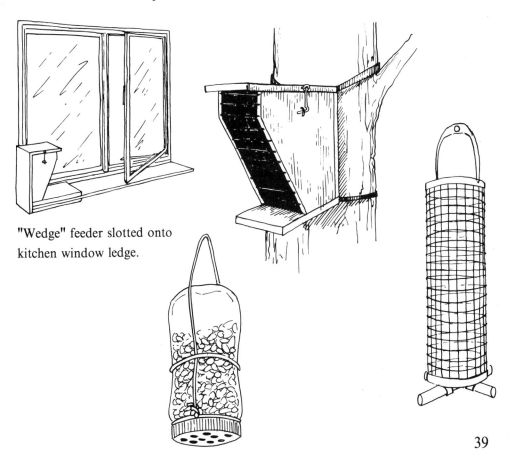

"Wedge" feeder slotted onto kitchen window ledge.

Nuts

Peanuts attract the tits, greenfinch, nuthatch, siskin, even the great spotted woodpecker, as well as the inevitable house sparrow. Bought in bulk they are less expensive; beware the red plastic mesh bags which soon develop holes through which the nuts will 'disappear' very quickly. Look for the 'we're safe nuts' stamp supported by RSPB and BTO; you can be sure these are free of the poison Aflotoxin found in some inferior peanuts. Unshelled peanuts strung up on a length of string or wire give excellent entertainment value as the tits extract kernels from within. Try walnuts, hazelnuts and Brazil nuts too, though you may need to crack the shells a little. When crops are good, you could collect nuts from woodland in autumn to save money.

Fruit

Try fruits of any kind, both the fleshy part and the seeds inside. Thrushes like rotting apples, and if you can save some until hard frosts and snow render soil invertebrates out of reach, you may attract redwings and fieldfares. You could prune branches of berberis, rowan, hawthorn etc., dry and store them in a cool, mouse-proof place, and then bring them out, branch by branch, when those left on the bushes run out. In really hard weather, check through the cupboard for out-of-date dried fruits such as currants, raisins, prunes and apricots, soak them overnight, and these too will be welcomed.

Hang half a coconut in a tree for tits, nuthatches and woodpeckers until all the hard white kernel is pecked off; then fill the shell with bird cake.

Seeds

Seeds are preferred by most finches, sparrows and buntings. Pet shops usually stock a selection. With luck, a skylark or meadow pipit might be attracted to smaller seeds such as hemp spread on the ground, but also try a hopper which releases just a few seeds at a time. A local farmer may let you have sweepings from his grain store; certainly the greenfinches will be thankful.

Of course, one free source of seed is the garden plants left specifically for this purpose; even plants like the much-maligned dock will, if left alone, yield a full head of seed ideal for a hungry bullfinch.

Kitchen scraps

Virtually all waste food from the house is good bird food. Assorted crusts, old cake, stale cheese, bacon rind, uncooked pastry, leftover cooked potatoes, rice and pasta, marrowbones and any cooked meats will do.

Bird Cake

Even solid fats can be used. Suet or dripping for example can be simply skewered and hung out, spread into rough bark of a tree or pressed into pine cones or purpose-made 2-3 cm diameter holes drilled into a hanging log. Better still, make a bird cake:

Melt fat in an old pan, add seeds, grated cheese, crushed biscuits, bread crumbs, oatmeal or almost anything available. Pour the mixture into moulds to set before hanging out. Plant pots and coconut shells work just as well as shop-bought 'bell' feeders.

Some Winter Visitors - helping them survive

In severe weather, hunger is usually the killer, not the weather itself.
Provide food regularly; clear a patch of snow, or use a board if necessary.

Fieldfare
*Prefers open areas and soil-living
invertebrates, but also berries of hawthorn,
holly and rowan. Fond of rotten apples.*

Waxwing
*Eats berries from rowan,
berberis, cotoneaster, hawthorn,
holly etc., rarely fruit or nuts
from bird table.*

Reed Bunting
*Takes mixed seeds,
pastry, bread and
cake from the ground.*

Brambling
*Occasionally visits gardens to
take mixed seed or bread and fat.*

Redwing
*As fieldfare, but
more timid, so hide fruit
under shrubs or hedge.*

Siskin
*Prefers alder and birch
seeds, but also peanuts.
Occasionally old fat, cheese,
coarse oatmeal and seeds.*

Nest boxes

To witness the first flight of a brood of blue tits reared on insects living in your own garden, in a nest box made and positioned by yourself, is a great joy. This is especially so if you have watched the process of courtship, nest-building, mating, incubation and feeding of the young. But first you need a nest box.

Several boxes are described in this chapter. Of these the blue-tit-type small-hole box is most successful. In design the most important aspects are the diameter of the hole, and the depth of the box below the hole (beware some garden centre boxes!). In its location the main things to avoid are cats and the heat of the summer sun on a south-facing wall. Other walls often make excellent sites for tit boxes as these birds need a clear flight path to and from the box. These same boxes are often used by single tits or perhaps dozens of wrens in winter for night-time roost sites.

The open-fronted box is perhaps the next design to try; it is easier to make since you need not use a drill and the roof is simply nailed on. However, such boxes are less often used. Try hiding the box in the thickest, prickliest, most inaccessible bush or climbing plant you have, since robins, the most likely inhabitants, prefer a well-hidden nest site.

Almost any wood of suitable size and strength is acceptable: softwood, plywood, second-hand floor boards etc., and the dimensions should be varied to suit available timber. Preservatives can be applied to prolong the life of the box so long as the nesting season is avoided; residual odours seem not to affect the birds. Competent carpenters should consider drilling holes in the base to aid drainage! A metal plate fitted around the entrance hole of a small-hole box gives some protection against marauding squirrels and woodpeckers.

Nesting Material

Offer the box 'unfurnished', as the birds will want to build their own nest.
However, do try providing dry grass, pine needles, tiny roots, moss, feathers, dog or human hair, tissue and anything else which might find favour. Hang them in nut feeders, or spread them on the ground nearby. Then watch the antics of broody birds, each trying to feather its own nest to perfection.

Disturbance

Excessive disturbance by people, cats, dogs, squirrels, magpies and crows causes the desertion of very many garden nests each year. However, most garden birds build at least three nests during a single summer, and success with only one or two broods will maintain the local population. Tits are unusual in that they lay all their eggs in one nest, timed so that the young fly in June when caterpillars are most plentiful. Only if a nest fails at an early stage will they try again, probably with a smaller clutch.

Many incubating birds sit tight as people walk by, and once the young have hatched the urge to care for them is very strong. However, only watch nesting birds if you can do so without disturbing them: from inside the house, from a distance or perhaps whilst sitting quietly apparently looking the other way!
Never approach a nest closely when the young seem nearly ready to leave. Such nestlings may 'explode', jumping down to the ground despite being unable to fly, almost certainly to be caught by a local cat. Ask the BTO about their Nest Record Scheme if you would like to contribute to a country-wide study.

Cleaning

Remove nesting material from a nest box in the autumn only if you are sure the birds have finished with the nest, and remember that a few young do return to roost for one or two nights after flying. Earwigs and other minibeasts often congregate in nest boxes, even empty ones. Indeed, old nests are the ancestral home of the clothes moth whose caterpillars eat the remains of feathers left behind by nestlings. Of greater danger is that parasites overwinter in nesting material ready to infect adult or young birds the following spring; use of a mild disinfectant in a cleaned-out box is worth considering.

Other nest sites

Finches, thrushes and wrens may nest in a bundle of twiggy branches strapped to a tree trunk, and robins may choose an old teapot (spout down for drainage) within a climbing plant. Plant pots, half coconut shells, shelves, old tins and even coat pockets may all suffice. Consider leaving the shed door ajar, or perhaps cutting a bird-sized hole near the top, but do make sure that no-one can imprison the residents.

cm   cm

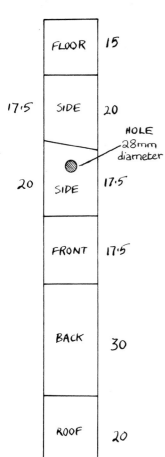

FLOOR	15
SIDE	20
SIDE	17·5
FRONT	17·5
BACK	30
ROOF	20

17·5 (SIDE height)

20 (SIDE height)

HOLE 28mm diameter

15 cm

Nest box designs

Small-hole nest box
Species: Mostly blue and great tit, but also coal tit, house sparrow, tree sparrow and nuthatch.
Materials: Plank about 120 cm x 15 cm x 15-20 mm
12 or more oval nails 35 mm long
2 staples and 6 cm flexible wire for catch
9 or more carpet tacks and piece of roofing felt, rubber or flexible plastic 15 x 8 cm for hinge
2 flat-headed nails, about 7 cm long to fix box in position. Use screws on walls.

Siting: Open position 2 - 6 m off ground on wall, shed, tree trunk or even a bare pole.

House Martin nest cup
To attract house martins, buy artificial nest cups; look for advertisements in bird magazines (e.g. RSPB's 'Birds'). They hook or screw to the timber beneath the eaves and are best positioned in groups unless house martins are already nesting close by. DIY nest cups can be made from pottery clay or a cement-sawdust mixture using half a children's plastic ball as a mould. The depth of the entrance hole should be no more than 25mm to exclude house sparrows. Offensive droppings on windows below can be intercepted by a temporary board fixed above the window. If necessary, deter sparrows by hanging nuts and bolts on strings some 23 cm long, 6 cm apart and 15 cm from the entrance.

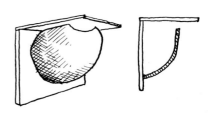

Small Open-fronted nest box

Species: Mostly robin, but also wren, blackbird (if box is large enough). Pied wagtail and spotted flycatcher if sited amongst climber on wall.

Materials: Plank about 120 cm x 15 cm x 15-20 mm

14 or more oval nails 35 mm long

2 flat-headed nails, about 7 cm long to fix box in position. Use screws on walls.

Siting: Conceal amongst thick vegetation, 1.5 - 3 m off ground. Walls covered by climbers ideal.

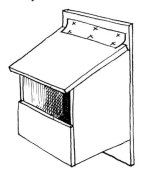

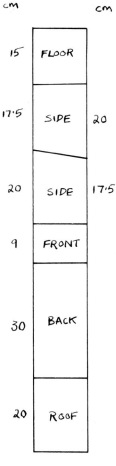

Large-hole nest box

Species: Starling, jackdaw, perhaps stock dove, little owl and great spotted woodpecker.

Construction: Made along the same lines as the small-hole and small open-fronted boxes, but much larger: about 20 cm square and 45 cm deep. The hole can be about 10 x 15 cm

Siting: High on a wall or tree.

Swallow nest cup

Purchase ready-made cups or make them yourself as for the house martin. Half coconut shells and small shallow trays also work. Fix to a wall or an exposed beam inside a porch, garage or farm outbuilding, where access for the birds is continuous throughout the breeding season.

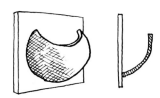

Swift box

Species: Block hole at start of season to exclude starlings and house sparrows before swifts arrive in late May.

Materials: Plank 1.5 m x 20 cm x 2 cm

24 or more oval nails 35 mm long

2 staples and 6 cm flexible wire for catch

9 or more carpet tacks and piece of roofing felt, rubber or flexible plastic 20 x 7 cm for hinge

Hooks or screws for fixing in position.

Siting: Under eaves of house 4 m or more off ground. By careful removal of a brick or section of wood from eaves, the box can be sited within loft. Swifts tend to be colonial so try two or more together.

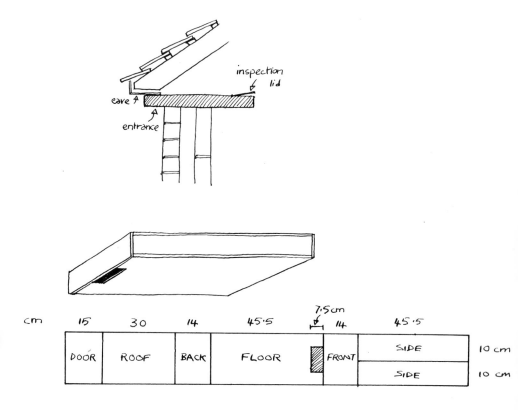

One last thought on nesting birds: the house martin, swallow and swift are undoubtedly much dependent on man-made structures for nest sites. Without people their populations would be much reduced.

Appendix I Common Garden Birds

Species	Notes
Blackbird	common resident of most gardens
Blackcap	summer visitor from Africa, April-October, some overwinter
Black-headed Gull	fearful of enclosed gardens, but takes chunks of food
Blue Tit	common resident, the most frequent nest box inhabitant
Bullfinch	common resident, eats buds in winter
Carrion Crow	resident, though shy, omnivorous (incl. birds' eggs)
Chaffinch	common resident, regular at ground feeding stations
Coal Tit	resident, likes conifers
Collared Dove	first nested in Britain 1955, now very common
Dunnock	common resident of most gardens
Feral Pigeon	descended from escaped racing pigeons
Goldcrest	resident, often overlooked due to small size, likes conifers
Goldfinch	resident, best known for liking of thistle seeds
Great Spotted Woodpecker	resident, regular at bird tables near woodland
Great Tit	common resident, aggressive bird table feeder
Greenfinch	common resident, relishes peanuts
House Martin	summer visitor from Africa, April-October
House Sparrow	very common resident, largely dependent on people
Jackdaw	resident, nests in colonies in holes, even in chimneys
Jay	resident of more wooded areas, fond of acorns
Linnet resident	may join other finches eating seeds
Long-tailed Tit	resident, flocks from June to February
Magpie	increasingly common in gardens, omnivorous (incl. birds' eggs)
Mistle Thrush	resident but less numerous than Song Thrush
Nuthatch	resident, regular at bird tables near woodland
Pied Wagtail	resident, most likely to visit town gardens in winter
Redpoll	resident, fond of birch and alder seeds in winter
Redwing	winter visitor from Scandinavia and beyond, visits gardens mostly in hard weather
Robin	common resident, the gardener's friend
Siskin	mostly a winter visitor from N.E. Europe, likes peanuts
Spotted Flycatcher	summer visitor from Africa, May-October
Song Thrush	common resident of most gardens
Starling	very common resident, also winter visitor from N. Europe
Swallow	summer visitor from S. Africa, April-September
Swift	summer visitor from Africa, May-July
Tawny Owl	resident, food includes birds, rodents and earthworms
Treecreeper	resident but often overlooked, prefers large trees
Willow Warbler	summer visitor from Africa, April-September
Woodpigeon	'Ring Dove', becoming more common and bold in gardens
Wren	common resident of most gardens, loud song

Appendix II Contacts for further information

Royal Society for the Protection of Birds (RSPB), The Lodge, Sandy, Beds. SG19 2DL
Also Young Ornithologists Club (YOC) for children

Royal Society for Nature Conservation (RSNC), The Green, Witham Park, Waterside South, Lincoln LN5 7JR. The national association of the County Wildlife Trusts. Also WATCH, the national wildlife and environment club for children.

British Trust for Ornithology (BTO), The Nunnery, Nunnery Place, Thetford, Norfolk IP24 2PU.

Appendix III Suppliers *Please send s.a.e. for catalogue.*

Suppliers of wildflowers seeds and plants

School Garden Company, P.O. Box 49, Spalding, Lincs. PE11 1NZ. Tel (0775) 769518 (Wildflower seeds, Books, Pond liners, Packs, Charts, etc.)

John Chambers, 15 Westleigh Road, Barton Seagrave, Kettering, Northants. NN15 5AJ

Emorsgate Seeds, Terrington Street, King's Lynn, Norfolk, PE34 4NT

Henry Doubleday Research Association, 20 Convent Lane, Bocking, Braintree, Essex

Stapeley Water Gardens Ltd., London Road, Stapeley, Nantwich, Cheshire, CW57JL

Natural Surroundings, Bayfield Estate, Holt, Norfolk NR25 7JN

Suppliers of bird food, feeders and tables

Wildbird Foods Ltd., The Rea, Upton Magna, Shrewsbury SY4 4UB

John Haith, Park Street, Cleethorpes, South Humberside DN35 7NF

RSPB (address on p.47)

Appendix IV Selected Book List

Bird books

Soper T. 1989, The Bird Table Book, David & Charles
Burton R. 1990, The RSPB Birdfeeder Handbook, Dorling Kindersley
Glue D. 1982, The Garden Bird Book, Macmillan
RSPB Bird Studies for Primary Science in the National Curriculum - for teachers
du Feu C. 1989, Nestboxes, BTO

Wildlife gardening guides from S G C Books - companions to this volume

Sibley B. 1989, Starting a Wildlife Pond
Cawdell P. 1987, Starting a Butterfly Garden
Thompson S. 1989, Bats in the Garden
Jones R. 1989, Developing your Playground
Gale D. 1987, Starting a School Garden
Starling A. & Loosley P. 1991, Wildflowers in the Garden

Other wildlife gardening books

Baines C. 1985, How to make a Wildlife Garden, Elm Tree Books
Hessayon D. 1990, The Biofriendly Gardening Guide, pbi publications

Identification guides

Hayman P. 1979, Mitchell Beazley Birdwatcher's Pocket Guide, Mitchell Beazley (one of very few good, truly pocket-sized bird identification books)
Chinery M. 1986, Collins Guide to the Insects of Britain and Europe, Collins
Carter D. 1979, The Observer's Book of Caterpillars, Warne
Rose F. 1991, The Wild Flower Key, Warne